Odysseus
and the
Cyclops

Retold by Nancy O'Connor

Illustrated by Roberto Barrios Angelelli

Flying Start
to Literacy®

Contents

Prologue   4

Chapter 1
An unknown land   8

Chapter 2
A walking nightmare   14

Chapter 3
Putting the plan into action   20

Chapter 4
A clever escape   26

A note from the author   32

Prologue

Thousands of years ago, in ancient Greece, a great war was fought between the Greeks and the Trojans. The war raged for ten long years, and many soldiers died. A clever and brave Greek prince named Odysseus came up with a plan to end the conflict. His soldiers built a giant wooden horse. The horse was hollow inside, and when it was built, Odysseus and his soldiers took their weapons and hid inside. The rest of the Greek army pretended to give up. They burnt their camp and sailed away.

When the Trojans saw that the Greeks had left, they believed the war was over. And when they saw the giant horse standing outside the city walls, they thought it was a gift. Joyfully, they opened the gates and hauled it inside. After a night of great revelry to celebrate the end of the war, everyone fell asleep. It was then that Odysseus and his soldiers crept out from their clever hiding place and attacked the unsuspecting Trojans. They overwhelmed the citizens of Troy and won the war.

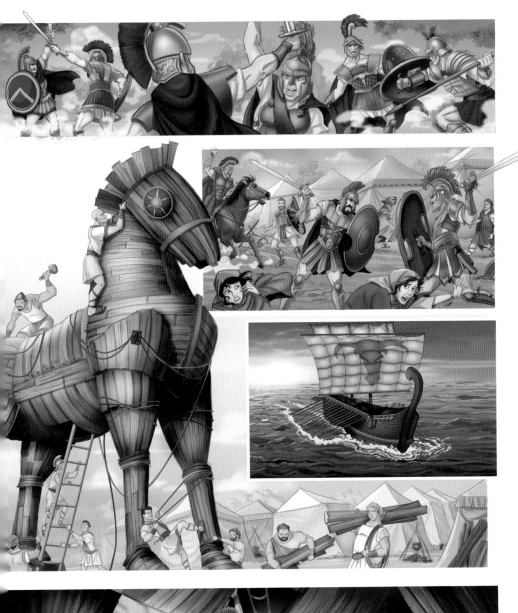

Odysseus and his soldiers should have gone straight home afterwards. Instead, they ransacked the city, destroying buildings and temples. They plundered and stole everything of value.

The gods watched all this and became enraged, especially at the destruction of their temples. They decided to punish the hero of the war, Prince Odysseus, and his soldiers.

When the victorious army finally began their homeward journey, the gods sent terrible storms down upon them. Some ships were blown far off course. Others were shipwrecked on rocky shores. The ship on which Odysseus and his soldiers sailed was lost at sea for months and months. He and his men began to starve. They were certain they would all die.

Chapter 1

An unknown land

Odysseus stood at the ship's railing, exhausted and discouraged. The once fine uniforms of his men were in tatters. Their beards were long, and their faces were thin from thirst and hunger. The men had served Odysseus well in the Trojan War, and he wanted to deliver them safely back to their families. But the gods continued to punish them, sending fierce winds, pelting rain and high seas. Only twelve of his soldiers were still alive. What was he going to do? He scanned the horizon in desperation.

"Look, men!" Odysseus suddenly shouted. He couldn't believe his eyes. "I see land in the distance!" The soldiers gathered around him, staring at the far-off beach where waves crashed on the rocks. The soldiers were uncertain about landing in such a treacherous place. They did not know where they were, but Odysseus persuaded them that it was their only chance of surviving.

"We have no choice," he said. "We must go ashore in this unknown land before our ship becomes completely wrecked and we starve to death. I am certain we will find food and water there. The only thing we have left to drink now is this half-empty wine skin," Odysseus said.

He slapped his men on their backs, and everyone agreed. They cheered and Odysseus began to steer the ship towards the land.

As soon as Odysseus and his men set foot on the beach, they began to explore the unfamiliar place. The island was rugged and windswept. They saw no signs of life anywhere, and sadly, they found no plants or animals they could eat. Tall grasses swayed in the wind, but that was all.

"Once again, the gods have abandoned us," one soldier complained. "This land is barren."

"It seems we will starve on land instead of at sea, but we will die just the same," said another.

"We fought bravely for you, Odysseus, and we trusted you to protect us," said a third.

"Don't give up hope," Odysseus said. "Those cliffs above us are dotted with caves. Let's take shelter in one and consider our options."

They climbed a rocky trail to the mouth of a huge cavern. Before they entered, Odysseus held up his hand and stopped the men. They stood quietly and listened. Was the place inhabited? Was someone lying in wait for them inside, ready to attack?

At first, they thought the sound they heard was the wind whistling through the grass. But, no, that was not it at all! Coming from inside the cave was the sound of bleating sheep!

Odysseus and the soldiers rushed inside and were amazed by what they found. Herds of lambs and goats filled the huge cave. Great rounds of cheese were piled on stone shelves. Jugs of fresh milk stood nearby. The mouths of the starving men began to water.

"Who does this food belong to?" one soldier asked. "Can we eat it?"

"It doesn't matter whose food it is," declared Odysseus. "Everyone knows the polite thing to do is care for the needs of visitors. Are we not visitors? Let us feast on this bounty!"

The men found a stack of wood and built a roaring fire. Then they slaughtered and roasted a lamb. "The smell is making me dizzy with hunger," a soldier cried. When the roast had turned golden brown, they gathered round and cut off sizzling chunks with their knives and swords. Juice dripped down their chins, as they hungrily gobbled up the meat.

"Nothing has ever tasted so delicious," said one of the men, wiping his chin with the back of his hand. "Our luck has turned. We will survive. Thank you, Odysseus!" The soldiers cheered their leader.

Soon they all devoured the creamy cheese. Then they washed their meal down with the cold, sweet milk. When all had eaten their fill and their stomachs were bulging, the soldiers stretched out by the warm fire and fell asleep. Once again, Odysseus had saved them.

Then the ground began to shake.

Chapter 2

A walking nightmare

Rumbling sounds came from outside the cave. The men woke suddenly and leapt to their feet in fear. At the entrance, there appeared the most monstrous creature they had ever seen. It was a giant, taller than any tree, with fists as large as boulders. A string of animal bones hung from his massive neck, and he wore animal skins and high leather boots on his huge feet. The creature stank of sweat and rotten meat. When he lumbered inside, the men saw his face by the glow of the firelight. It was hideous, for he had but one eye, right in the centre of his forehead.

One of the soldiers shouted, "Tell me, please, that I am having a nightmare!" But the others cried out in fear, "No, we see it, too!"

Odysseus knew immediately who the giant was. He had heard tales of this fearsome creature. He was the most famous Cyclops. His name was Polyphemus.

"What are you doing in my home?" bellowed the Cyclops. "Why have you eaten all my food?"

The men cowered in the shadows, trembling. Brave Odysseus spoke up. "We are strangers in this land and our ship is wrecked on your shore, Polyphemus," he said.

The soldiers stared at one another in confusion. "Our ship is not wrecked," one whispered to another.

His companion put a finger to his lips. "Hush! Odysseus knows what he is doing."

"What do I care if you have shipwrecked on my island?" growled Polyphemus.

"Do you not believe in offering hospitality to visitors?" asked Odysseus.

"Bah!" roared Polyphemus. "Visitors bring gifts. What have you brought me? Nothing!" Then he reached out his huge arms and grabbed a soldier in each fist. "These men would make nice gifts!" And without further ado, he ate both men, bones and all.

The soldiers stared at the monster in shock and horror. "Do something," a soldier whispered to Odysseus.

"We must make a plan," he whispered back. "We will wait until the Cyclops goes to sleep and then slip by him and escape."

But Polyphemus must have heard the men, because he went to the entrance of the cave and rolled an enormous stone across it, blocking the way out. Then the monster lay down in front of the stone, burped loudly and fell asleep.

Odysseus didn't sleep a wink. His men were counting on him to save them. He sat with his back against the stone wall, trying to think of a solution to their predicament.

When the first rays of morning sun peeped through the cracks around the stone in the mouth of the cave, Polyphemus awoke. He sat up and stretched. When he saw Odysseus and his men, his ugly face lit with a mean smile.

"I always like a good breakfast before I take my sheep and goats out to graze on the hillsides," Polyphemus said. He stood up, and moving faster than any of them could have imagined, he snatched up two more soldiers, one in each fist. Without further ado, he shoved them into his mouth and ate them, bones and all.

Then Polyphemus stared at Odysseus with his one fierce eye and he shook his giant fist. "Do not think you can escape. I plan to eat your men, two by two, but I will save you for last," he said. Then he rounded up his sheep and goats and drove them outside. And, before he left, he rolled the heavy stone across the opening once again. The men were trapped.

"What will we do?" one soldier cried out. "I did not fight bravely in a great war to end up being eaten for dinner by some hideous beast."

Odysseus looked at his frightened men and declared, "I have a plan."

Chapter 3

Putting the plan into action

Gathering his remaining eight men together, Odysseus said, "We must get to work while the Cyclops is away. Bring me that great log in the corner."

He instructed his men to pick up their swords and knives and sharpen the log to a point. They worked for hours, for the log was huge. When Odysseus was satisfied that it was sharp enough, he had the men put the tip of the spear into the fire to harden it. "A perfect weapon to use on a Cyclops. Good job, men. Now hide our spear deep in the shadows."

Then they sat and waited.

Late in the afternoon, the ground began to shake, and the men knew the Cyclops had returned. Polyphemus rolled back the stone and drove his herd of animals inside. He quickly blocked the opening once again and turned to his uninvited visitors.

"I'm hungry," he said. "I've worked hard all day, and I want my supper." The soldiers trembled in fear. They knew what was going to happen next. But brave Odysseus stepped forward and raised his hand.

"Wait a moment, Polyphemus. Would you like some wine with your supper?" Odysseus asked. "The only thing we have left from our ship is this wine skin. And very fine wine it is. No other man will ever bring you better, since you are such an unkind host." Odysseus held the wine skin up high for the Cyclops to see.

The giant snatched the skin away from Odysseus and gulped down the wine. Then he began to roar with laughter. "This is, indeed, fine wine. Now tell me your name so that I might properly thank you for it."

"I am Nobody," Odysseus replied.

"That's a strange name," Polyphemus said. "But thank you, Nobody, for the delicious wine. Now I am ready for my dinner." In the blink of his one eye, Polyphemus grabbed two more unlucky soldiers. Without further ado, he ate them up, bones and all. Then the giant burped loudly, slouched against the wall and fell into a deep sleep.

Odysseus and his few remaining men waited until the Cyclops was snoring loudly. Then, with a finger to his lips, Odysseus motioned to the soldiers to help him pick up the sharpened log. They hoisted their spear onto their shoulders and pointed it at the sleeping giant.

At that very moment, the Cyclops snorted and stirred. The men froze where they stood, eyes wide, terrified he would awaken. But soon the snoring began again, even louder than before.

"All together now," Odysseus whispered. He and the soldiers raced across the cave and thrust the point of the spear deep into the eye of the Cyclops, blinding him.

Polyphemus stumbled to his feet, screaming in rage and pain. He pulled the spike from his eye and thrashed around, trying to grab the men, but they quickly scrambled out of his reach.

"Arrrgggh!" he yelled. "Help me! Help me!" His cries echoed throughout the cave. Other Cyclopes who lived in the hills nearby heard his cries of agony and came running.

"What is going on in there?" his friends shouted. "What ails you, Polyphemus?"

When he heard his friends outside, Polyphemus roared, "Nobody is hurting me!"

"If nobody is hurting you, why are you shouting?" one yelled back.

"My eye! My eye!" Polyphemus cried out.

"What has happened to your eye?" shouted another Cyclops.

"Nobody did this to me!" Polyphemus raged.

Outside, his Cyclopes friends looked at each other in puzzlement, and scratched their giant heads. "If nobody is hurting him, let us go back to sleep," one said, and so they all returned to their caves.

Finally, Polyphemus fell to the ground, unconscious. It was time for Odysseus to put the final part of his plan into action.

Chapter 4

A clever escape

When the first rays of morning sun once again peeped through the cracks around the stone at the entrance to the cave, the blind Cyclops awoke in a fury.

"I will get you all," he bellowed. "You will not escape me." He rolled away the stone and stood with his arms outstretched across the opening so that he could feel if any of the soldiers tried to creep past him.

But during the night, Odysseus and his six soldiers had gathered the biggest sheep and, two by two and side by side, used rope they had found to tie them together. Odysseus instructed his men tie themselves to the sheep. Then the sheep could carry them out of the cave, right under Polyphemus's nose.

As the sheep stepped out into the sunlight, Polyphemus patted each of them carefully to make sure no man was hiding among them. He never imagined the men might be underneath the animals.

When Odysseus and his men were safely out of the cave and away from the reach of the Cyclops, they crawled from under the sheep and raced for the cliff. They scrambled down the rocky path to the beach. Then they pushed their ship back into the sea and leapt aboard. Soon the wind filled the sails. The men were jubilant. They had escaped!

Odysseus stood on the deck and shouted up at the giant stumbling along the top of the cliff. "Polyphemus, it was I, Prince Odysseus, who outwitted you. I am the one who put out your eye. There will be no more Greek soldiers for you to eat!"

But Odysseus should have kept his mouth shut. He should never have taunted the Cyclops. His pride got in the way of his good judgement.

"Odysseus, you will pay for this!" Polyphemus screamed. He lifted a giant boulder over his head and flung it into the ocean. Huge waves rose up, nearly capsizing the ship.

When Polyphemus' father, Poseidon, God of the Ocean, heard how Odysseus had blinded his son, he, too, became enraged. He rose up from the depths right in front of Odysseus's ship. His sea-blue eyes flashed in fury and water streamed from his long sea-blue hair. Shaking his giant trident at the terrified men huddled on the deck, he shouted, "I curse you forever, Odysseus." Lightning flashed and the winds began to howl. "You will long regret what you have done to my son." Then the God of the Ocean disappeared back into the sea.

And, indeed, Prince Odysseus came to regret his actions. His journey home to Ithaca took ten more years. He suffered hardship after hardship – from thunderbolts and shipwrecks, to whirlpools and cannibals, and the last of his loyal soldiers died along the way.

The brave hero of the Trojan War learnt two valuable lessons on his long journey – when you've won the war, you should just go home, and bragging is never a good idea . . . especially to a Cyclops.

A note from the author

I remember reading a children's version of Greek myths when I was in Year 5. I had a teacher who loved mythology and encouraged her students to learn the names of the Olympian gods and goddesses and what they each represented. There were so many that it was a daunting task. Zeus, Athena and Poseidon weren't too hard to remember, but I had to make up techniques to memorise some of the others. Sixty years later I can still recall the goddess of "hearth and home – Hestia".

Back then, I never imagined I'd one day be asked to retell the exciting and rather gruesome myth of Odysseus and the Cyclops. It has been fun to revisit the adventures of the Trojan War and its hero. I love how Odysseus outwits the monster, showing that brains can prevail over brawn. I also love the lesson he learnt about the dangers of boasting. Can you think of another story where boasting gets a character into trouble?